Copyright (c) 2020 by Humor Heals Us. All rights reserved. No part of this book may be reproduced in any form without permission in writing from the publisher. Please send bulk order requests to Humorhealsus@gmail.com Printed and bound in the USA
978-1-953399-04-5 Humorhealsus.com

Artsy Fartsy the Penguin
and the Farting Wars

by Humor Heals Us

Follow us on FB and IG @humorhealsus
To vote on new title names and freebies, visit us at humorhealsus.com for more information.

📷 @humorhealsus

📘 @humorhealsus

www.ingramcontent.com/pod-product-compliance
Lightning Source LLC
Chambersburg PA
CBHW042316280426
43673CB00081B/398